Martine, dearest colleague:

What a delight ~
I am really honored to send this off to you,
& I hope this message finds you enjoying
splendid summer!

VELA.

Your, with blessings,

KNAR GAVIN

MW01126225

the operating system c. 2019

the operating system digital print//document

VELA.

ISBN # 978-1-946031-64-8
copyright © 2019 by Knar Gavin
edited and designed by ELÆ [Lynne DeSilva-Johnson] with Orchid Tierney

For additional questions regarding reproduction, quotation, or to request a pdf for review
contact operator@theoperatingsystem.org

Print books from The Operating System are distributed to the trade by SPD/Small Press Distribution, with ePub and POD via Ingram, with production by Spencer Printing, in Honesdale, PA, in the USA. Digital books are available directly from the OS, direct from authors, via DIY pamplet printing, and/or POD.

This text was set in Steelworks Vintage, Europa-Light, Gill Sans, Minion, and OCR-A Standard.

<u>Cover Art</u> uses an image from "Collected Objects & the Dead Birds I Did Not Carry Home," by Heidi Reszies.

the operating system
www.theoperatingsystem.org
mailto: operator@theoperatingsystem.org

for my parents and each of their armadillos ...

CONTENTS

Catastrophe is always about to arrive again. We live in ruin's midst. We have always dwelt in this middle, at this doorway that sometimes holds firm against storm but sometimes blows open as the elements arrive.

— Jeffrey Jerome Cohen ("Elemental Relations")

A playful nip is not only not a bite, it is also not not a bite.

— Brian Sutton-Smith (*The Ambiguity of Play*)

HERACLITORUS

lit, dead. or sea'd, a live wire.

logos de cahier. logos de feu.

WOLF

pint after pint: utterly a lone wolf
for the knowledge of milk,
and what
it was.

at each corner
I meet the kitties of
dairy and the saucers really
do fly, rendered mammary running
off to story the high towers of industry.

into a book of cloves I bend
my howl yet am born back again, a sun-heaved
blockage among the growing shadows of morning.

CORN PAJAMAS, GREEN HOUSE GAS

After Timothy Morton

soundlessly move the plastic teeth
to close them up then sneak out.

who serves poetry liver
at this hour? our streets
are zippers of outering.

Möbius, mopey pus. 2-way
teeth & hyper objectionable.
are we in the toxic yet?

please: let something
dark happen to me in the night.
I am red into the LD50 of this text.

these clouds are only so much
caught-on clogging the soundscape.

my acrid tongue sticks
with fiber, regular glass.

f/unearth: scrape me with your face as it grows out.
forgive the dilating frame for this margin of air.

Polly, Ethel: lean loves livest now and leaning yet.
twin spines bent back on themselves.

AFTER MATSUBAYASHI'S *HORSES OF FUKUSHIMA*

radio horse singing to radio horse
   ultrasonic bodies gone full voice
& knowable to no living tongue.

     maybe it is as
cixous says: we are just big enough to cry
  for a dog, but never big enough to cry for our mother.

maybe the horses are like the kids, & the eggs
  & art: we non-recognize them — move to-
ward them from a point of non-view.

this perspective is

the perspective from the shore
  of radio waves
of slower-than-light

   none of us has gone full-radio lately
not in my neighborhood,
     & not in my mother's.

for now i water the screen of my eyes, salt slicking to grow
  a temporary memorial for body of horse, & dog's body,
& notherly dove of world piece alit in my blazing palm.

PORCINE STRESS SYNDROME

I've become an arched thing

        broom handled red
        over time

or a loss
        of the capacity to keep
   a room

debris

    is one form of surround.

        I began with a sousname
and that's what I'll keep

   beneath me there is much air

the arch of my back

        matches on
        graphic ally

to the bananas
of a broken world

system which may
          or may not be dying

                    .

     It's June. The bugs in my
anus are screaming. My

children are breathless
some days like early cinema

  as the real clicks into place.

Punches a hole in the ticket
  to let the animals inside. The
vary skin suit that lets me ride
        down on the (s)laughter
              and its many houses,
        each glistening carefully.

I meet her
on the porch.

Again, she's done it: sprung from below
in a shake of clay from wing to land

on my porch railing bearing
a broad mute face and twin bulbs for eyes.

Dear Cade (may I call you that?), It-bizarre
you've been here all along in sci-fi glimmer
armored amidst holey shifted earth.

Not some weird bloom from the Anthropocene but
older than that human vestigial, the appendix, so many
editions of which have already gone off to scrap.

What did you call me
at the beginning of things?

How did you ring, and did you do it?
Tissue the summons, songue besting my ear.

HOMO-COGNITARIAT

    —quick-listed
to the longhand of playbor

I lost in border
parts a country—quick of
the nail and bitten through—

what will it have been, to have played?

I confess no green
flower—No, am wooden flower

    as in

wish I hadn't

a slow leak
can happen in a bicycle
tube—inside a girl—
inside a tube inside a girl

    so I confess:

I know now it

is possible to be at once
full and empty
and so do
confess

this: a flattening—

(yes, *property is a measure of elimination*)

—now to limn red fessing up to
no flower to snuff: the brutal ex
-hibit, the habit I, aye

VULTURE

I've been
thinking
in them

this currency
a weather one wills
vultures

they arrive
smalled by great
capes of meat

slowed as
a violence
congealed

ancestral task force or
the dinosaur inside
today, they are
our final fleet
assistants

charged with public mourning
they bow over the mealing dead
help the flatlands up to haunt

soon we will all be vultures, amateurish
amongst spoils of the present

the dead can fly
& they're doing it

scrap-meal stowaways
inside bellies to scour
the land, houring it

with screech.

VOGELFREI

I bought my worm and I
my worm become.

This is true for you also.

Look on the apple field:
it writhes with us.

Applecider,
fratricider.

The numb sweet juice,
The numb and sweetened tongue.

APOLOGY TO A PLANET

I want to be a machine.
—Andy fucking Warhol

I have been willed to what will have been. Say someday meets
someday heading to coming from. Say there is another world. Say
it is this one. It may be true: the intimacy of self-representation
occludes even as it reveals.

                    I've used black tape to tape winter
reeds to my wall. I've taped a shitting ass to my wall. It was
a gift. I've taped a gift to my wall. I have one color copy and one
black & white facsimile. Like the hands with their way of running
over walls and overalls, the hardest to remove.

                              As if
you could really cover it all. As if the reed weren't a strangle
of dried berries, each shrunken balloon attesting to a clot.

Once I knew a guy yes-man enough, yes, I heard once
how to be "buck up, Kiddo" for real. Let's follow the path
of crushed figs: we will name our horses Cookie & Brownie
and we will ride insulin-high into the West.

                          In the West, a metal
raises a metal. I raise the metal to my mouth. I shake hands
with Andy Warhol. Once sucked the war-hole like I needed it.

Say someday meets someday heading to coming from.
Say there is another world. Tell me it is this one.

MISS TRACTION

I found you inside culture
running your hands against
its housed-glassily, peering
into its out-side, which was
your won and ownly face.

Still, you've become my lv-object.

I bring you
poems of dwindling.

I bring you
our final apple.

I bring you orchestraws and a most earie drink.

THE OPENING YARD

For other silent kinder gardeners

I was led once split
in the lip to the nurse's gloves
and though my speech frothed
with blood, it was the hands
she wanted and for the blisters
there, an ointment; a gauze.

I would to the grounds
of play go to monkey again
among the green gripping
hard through the yellowing
wrap, mouth hung just
open, its tear of flesh
beading a reddening globe—
sun-sprung jewel for those later
days when my eyes would make
contact and I should, aching, speak.

But, there's no helping the mouth, so
harden these hands with speech made strange.

MOUTH

Phonemes am
bling over the thresh
old. I will hum a durge. I
will speak in meat or.

ART FROM WITHOUT:
CLOSENESS AS A NODAL MANIFESTATION

After Google

All I can think
of is my AI.

Somewhere, she is
writing a poem.

Somewhere, she's learning to bleed.

MOUTHS OF GRAIN

A samaritan? Just
a person from a place.

I too have
come from.

Have tried to be good when I pass
you on the road, your mouth a tear
across our pool of flesh, tiniest country.

I might swear—I'd like to—we set the sun, bone-illumed,
& cast it all river, my tear-maw to yours, flowing through the gape.

MONEY JUGS

This water under my skin
is not forever water.

It expends
through tiny holes
above the vapor slits,
out from the croc canals of
the pomegranate river running
off from the Cis-effusive mountain.

My sweet is saline now. Salt lick,
then lapped. I hate the television waves
lapping my grain. I hate the Teflon

that bastes the jewels
of my waters. I'm a new millennium,
what are you? Have you forgiven
the tabloids yet?

No one was supposed to know
about our serpent mother,
about where all of the eggs went.

Memory has forgotten to smear
the blood trail again.

In my next life, I'll leave truth
prints on everything, take
my ontos of contagion
and proffer it to the world.

What is aubergine
in me seeds
verdant. A ready

multitude I
unmanner and enter
the slopyard

where I lap
and am lapped,
shell and unshell.

Like sulfur so
cannon, detritus
heaving inexhaustible yolk.

ODE, HER

Neighbor-moms called me
fast paste, then flattened
their daughters
with irons, slow
pastures.

They chaffed into dust while
I, Mouth to the mega
hone, pursed, sucked
it in. Lashed lids with masc
ara—aria of hinge—the
sweeping doors of my
feathered wink. A real
looker, I look. Am also
looked back. And man

icure sometimes, with a swipe
of lacquer, fastest paste. The
liquor closet from which
I Spring. I snatch

the proverbial pooch out
from neighbor-mom's purse
and place fore
finger there on the meat

of the bitch-dog's hound
quarter—I press
down to move the whole
limb. In this history
of limning, I shine. I press
the extensor and the leg swings out.

TO ANN E CHOIC

Free from echo, why should I, myself.
Ana, you are not a nice girl.

How can you stay in that other room?
How can you dwell so far outside song?

Every egg is near-plant.

Be the egg. I mean
the chicken plant,
readying
to live a, sure,
mostly flightless

life. And yet.

To have wings:

after so
much white
and shell
and

endless wall.

POMEGRANATE

I spin my rounds, full
of sinister light

bulbs. Each socket flickers
red round crimson tooth.

I go through the bowels
of body like bones
through earth

all white nodes
unfleshed among shit
and yes, singing.

I played dead for a while.

Happily, my theater was small and
no one came looking. In my play

I ground every last swing set.
I ate the sand and sand became.

URCHIN

For sibling faces, beneath the water

out from
the maw of river
and amaranth
of animal
swell

I became,
swimless, a
bundle of urchin
middlemeat, suited
in spine and all
the more
heavy

the river
would have scatte
red me—run my
bones across its sandy
floor—had me live blind
that wet desert and its
storming—O, Death,
you did once near-
have me—had we

given to scattering
what a clamor!   a water
insisting orchestras

   my femur playing
vertebral lengths
  with skull
sluice to Onward,
   every orbital
singing

JETÉ

After Thelma & Louise

             have the thought to

                         move on to

                              the porch

                    yet a thing steps in

                           between

      outdoor lemon swell

                               nearly

           reaches us through the blinds

      they do say it

      I love you
      each way

as though every

each surrounded equally

something we are inside of if we are—

a hyperobject   a certain clam

two women in a car suspended

over the gulch   tongues waving

flags of origin

the lemon nearly reaches us

it is a planet
it is a throne in the world.

ACKNOWLEDGEMENTS

Grateful acknowledgments to the following publications in which some of these poems were first published, sometimes under different titles:

AGNI, "After Matsubayashi's *Horses of Fukushima*" and "Vulture"
Bayou, "Pomegranate"
Birdfeast, "Homo-Cognitariat"
Booth, "Urchin"
Bop Dead City, "After Wall"
Denver Quarterly Review, "Cicada"
Foundry, "My Desert Be Coming"
glitterMOB, "Money Jugs"
Heavy Feather Review, "Mouth"
The Journal, "Art from Without: Closeness as A Nodal Manifestation"
Pouch, "Ode, Her" and "Mouths of Grain"
Print-Oriented Bastards, "Apology to a Planet"
Quarterly West, "Vogelfrei"
Supplement, "Corn Pajamas, Green House Gas"

-

In "Homo-Cognitariat," I borrow the line *property is a measure of elimination* from C.S. Giscombe's *Prairie Style* (Dalkey Archive Press, 2008).

"*Vogelfrei*," imports the Marxian sense of the term *vogelfrei* ("bird-free"), which suggests a doubled freedom from both rights and property. Karl Marx invoked this term to describe the proletariat class as it emerged during the decline of feudalism in the late-fifteenth and early-sixteenth centuries in Western Europe.

AFTER-WORDS

METABOLIC MACHINES AND MATERIALS
A CONVERSATION WITH
KNAR GAVIN

Greetings! Thank you for talking to us about your process today!
Can you introduce yourself, in a way that you would choose?

Greetings! I am poet-theorist (or, perhaps, a maker-spectator/spectating-maker). I should admit, though—the writing/theorizing mode often has often felt rather contingent, and few of my processors work properly without mechanical (that, is bicycle) and organic assistance (gardening; nature-touching). I'm not not a cyborg! Beyond these things, I'm currently in pursuit of a doctoral degree in English at the University of Pennsylvania, and I study neocolonial media ecologies in poetry and new media.

Why are you a poet/writer/artist?

To tease that Donna Haraway cyborg thread a bit, I make things and seek to make-with whenever I can. C.S. Giscombe has written about how cooks and poets bear a certain relation, and that has always really resonated with me. Though I've found the makings-with of text to be especially enriching, the general tendency to cobble/nurture/enliven pervades my life in general (side-eying my garden/kombucha SCOBY hotel/bad paintings/ bicycle tube art). I want things (words included) to be themselves, yet I know this might mean that they must be(come) other things, too!

This is probably why I'm big on soups and stews—I privilege recovery (whether of vegetables or scraps of text) over discard, the blurring mélange over the clean edging of the parcel. Even within the poem, I often feel as though I'm hurrying to(-)ward something—trying to preserve a thing (or give it other word-comrades) even as it disappears.

When did you decide you were a poet/writer/artist (and/or: do you feel comfortable calling yourself a poet/writer/artist, what other titles or affiliations do you prefer/feel are more accurate)?

Ha! I rarely know what to call myself and I avoid it where I can. Insofar as the poet's existence is a peculiarly stunned one (I borrow this from C.D. Wright), I am very much a poet—the world is constant with its surprises, and I try to remain open to that, and to the sense that I might yet be addressed from a perspective I do not know, or cannot anticipate (that point of 'non-view' that comes up in "After Matsubayashi's Horses of Fukushima," *which I pirated from Hélène Cixous).*

As a kid (back then I thought, somehow, that I hated poetry!), I genuinely wanted to be a horse —all nostrils, ears, and muscle. Thinking about it now, that desire feels like a precursor of sorts; there's such reciprocity there, in horse-ness—even in being led the horse pulls off a certain manner of leading, and it's that active relation/dynamic tether that shores the group up against flight. Poetry does some of this led-leading, too, plus its sensorium is (or ought to be) huge, and horsey.

What's a "poet" (or "writer" or "artist") anyway? What do you see as your cultural and social role (in the literary / artistic / creative community and beyond)?

As my rather twining answers to previous questions may've revealed, I am into thinking in conversation with others—their ideas, how they sense and articulate the poetics of life—this feels so central to me, and to how I conceive of the maker (whatever the materials of their art or poetic practice might be). Setting aside the more toxic rivulets that all too often extend out from institutionalized forms of art-making, I am convinced creative communities of like maker-minds are often very good at equipping themselves with new means of accessing complex social, human problems (and, increasingly, their environmental correlatives). As a community member, I see my role as an amplificatory one; while I do produce work myself, a core component of my practice involves reading/viewing/sharing in the transmission of the works of others. This is a part of my ongoing effort to responsively (and responsibly!) engage with and really feel/appreciate the sorts of imperatives that those works are trying to advance. This is a reciprocal thing, too—I so appreciate being read, and I hope that some of my works spark contemplation and meaningful conversation about some of the crap that's going on in the world beyond the spines of our books.

To get at it differently, it feels probable that every poem is a poem that falls in the woods! From there, any poeming achieved has been made possible among and because of the trees and soil and animals, the microbes, air and rot—these condition the possibilities for what the poem might yet make, and become and demand (of the world, I suppose). The poem (or artwork) is as enriched and enriching as its context will allow it to be. This is part of why I so value the Operating System. Across the conglomerate of creators constellated by the press, there is a shared dedication to multi-form creation, critical thinking, and insistent inquiry. It's just this sort of variegated work that stands to extend beyond its enabling containers (the page/a given sonic environment/the classroom) and really get at the totality of pressures, vibrancies, and threats that imperil our planetary present.

Talk about the process or instinct to move these poems (or your work in general) as independent entities into a body of work. How and why did this happen? Have you had this intention for a while? What encouraged and/or confounded this (or a book, in general) coming together? Was it a struggle?

It really was a matter of instinct plus some trial and terror! When I began work on the chapbook, I drew together my poems that were most concerned with plant and animal life, yet a lot of the work, I realize now, relates also to capital and energy, to production and exhaustion. A bunch of these poems are trying to process where fecundity and appetite fit within our finite, unequally-shared world.

Did you envision this collection as a collection or understand your process as writing or making specifically around a theme while the poems themselves were being written / the work was being made? How or how not?

This body of work moved through a series of titles and poem combinations, beginning with Animal Lives, which then became Live Lives only to morph, finally, into Vela., the title it bears now. Both of my earlier titles contain polysemic doublets. With 'animal lives,' I was trying to get at the so-called 'animal' in general as well as the chimerical singularity of particular animals, which are never quite or never just animal (the human seems to alternate between crisscrossing through and nesting within this sprawling domain). In each preliminary title, there was an attempt to grapple with material being and its messy constitutive relations. I wanted to capture some of what the poems capture—an understanding of life in and as emergence—as something of an active (living and evolving) series (of singular lives).

What formal structures or other constrictive practices (if any) do you use in the creation of your work? Have certain teachers or instructive environments, or readings/writings/work of other creative people informed the way you work/write?

A lot of my creative practice involves sitting with (or riding my bike in the company of) a single thing and letting that thing become something else; shapes—semiotic ones perhaps especially—tend to shift beneath sustained attention, and I am interested in both instigating and excavating those shifts.

As for environments and writings of influence, I hardly know where to begin. In recent years, I've been really impacted by the works of Don Mee Choi, Yedda Morrison, and Allison Cobb; Muriel Rukeyser and Adrienne Rich have been big for me, too, and I don't know whether I'd even be writing poetry without Giscombe's Prairie Style, my first book-length poetry love. I am ever grateful to my earliest poetry mentors, Craig Dworkin, Shira Dentz, and Joyelle McSweeney especially, and I often find myself tracking back to insights offered by my colleagues at the Iowa Writers Workshop (2011-2013). Beyond these, I feel truly blessed to live in Philadelphia—it's such a poetry-wealthy city, and I feel lucky to have found my way into such a vibrant reading/writing community.

Speaking of monikers, what does your title represent? How was it generated? Talk about the way you titled the book, and how your process of naming (individual pieces, sections, etc.) influences you and/or colors your work specifically.

*Ultimately, I abandoned my earlier two-term monikers (*Animal Lives *succeeded by* Live Lives*) in favor of that single (and sentenced!) term* Vela.*, in part because of the multiplicity it designated (vela is the plural form of velum, 'veil'), while also suggesting shifting movements between concealment and revelation (the veil which itself reveals a further veil, a new valance billowing, or whatever). Velum is a botanical and mycological term that refers to a membranous, veil-like structure—refers, then, to the necessity of something remaining always partially obscured.*

I wanted to have that sense of layering and layered repetition while also suggesting a differentiating aspect, too, hence the sentencing period ('.') after Vela.*, which suggests a bundled thing, yet distinctly so—not all bundles are alike! I was also fascinated by the aural identity between velum and vellum (calf skin, used as parchment), though I'll leave that comment to float unelaborated—an invitation to reveal!*

As for individual poem titles, I tend to keep those simple, if I can (hence titles like "Mouth" and "Cicada"), yet some of them do get away from me, especially when my theory-bent thinking cuts in ("Homo-Cognitariat" and "Art from Without: Closeness as a Nodal Manifestation," for example).

What does this particular work represent to you ...as indicative of your method/creative practice? ...as indicative of your history? ...as indicative of your mission/intentions/hopes/plans?

These poems were composed over a five-year period. Though some are quite recent, many of them have existed in one form or another for several years. Some of the oldest ones were written during my time at Iowa. My MFA thesis involved this manuscript of "cycling-generated" poems called Cotor: Excerpts from Variable Roads, *but the poems that ended up in* Vela.

were different. They certainly shared air with the Cotor *project, but they were more focused, and, I guess, more obviously poem-like, and perhaps snappier, too (the* Cotor *work involves a lot of sprawling pieces and more overtly visual elements). Having shifted now into a more academic professional track, I am really surprised by the poems in* Vela. *as they seem to have anticipated—maybe even produced—my turn toward environmental media and eco-critical research.*

What does this book DO (as much as what it says or contains)?

Essaying "In Praise of Profanation," Agamben offers an interesting account of museumification: "everything today can become a Museum, because this term simply designates the exhibition of an impossibility of using, of dwelling, of experiencing." A book, importantly, is not a museum— at least not in the sense described here. My favorite books defy separability—they root around, and forage; they travel (sometimes just a few shards or memorized fragments at a time) and soil and find. Sometimes, such movements lead or lend toward new hands and new textual lives in/with/for other books. I hope Vela. *will do some of these things. I want it to be a useful book, and a pluripotent one too; an instrument of instrumentation (taking no object for itself) rather than instrumentalization. I hope this book will be one which both plays and puts things back in(to) play, and I hope some of its poems invite dwelling and offer refuge (so often, I have myself been supplied these things, in the shape of a poem).*

What would be the best possible outcome for this book? What might it do in the world, and how will its presence as an object facilitate your creative role in your community and beyond? What are your hopes for this book, and for your practice?

I think a lot about materials (literary; textual; physical; metaphysical) as media—where does the thing go, and between which things might an object navigate or, more vitally, negotiate? I have agonized a little bit over the household that is this chapbook—how did all of that get in there? A poem about getting sucked under a snag (that is, a big ole dead tree bit!) in one of Seattle's tributaries shares a spine with several about gender and violence, plus a dead ex haunts the white space of so many of these pages; that much makes sense, maybe—scary, denaturing natures, human-impactful and otherwise. But the book's full of critters and vegetables, too—the very stuff of subsistence.

This in mind, I imagine this book—as its best self—would proceed as a metabolic entity of sorts: to borrow from William c. Williams, "A poem is a small [or large] machine of words." Machines are things with metabolic jobs—they (t)ask the materials of their operations to be otherwise, or materialize differently. In the best of outcomes, these poems will be good machines, large or small; as for the small selection of more ecologically-invested and/or culturally critical poems, I hope they provoke useful lines of questioning and reflection.

Let's talk a little bit about the role of poetics and creative community in social and political activism, so present in our daily lives as we face the often sobering, sometimes dangerous realities of the Capitalocene. How does your process, practice, or work otherwise interface with these conditions?

I've been thinking quite a bit about those moments of heightened attention that become possible in aesthetic experiences; what happens after such moments, and how might we—as creators and, let's acknowledge the complicity, consumers of art and literature—move beyond those kinds of moments and into more active efforts to interface with this hostile, unjust, and increasingly ecologically unstable world?

I haven't fully metabolized these questions myself and perhaps that ought not be the point. What I can say is, I think we do have an obligation to speak beyond individual experience and to reach outward to the painful realities of the present; sometimes, this might entail amplifying a creative or critical insight we encounter in a work of art or poetry and letting it have a second (or third, or fourth) life in a more expressly activist context. These sorts of interventions can feel all too local, but I think it's important to remain heartened by the value of cultural production—the insights that come from creative output really are crucial, and open into a host of alternative forms of knowledge production, ones which might more adequately counter some of these capitalist/sexist/racist/xenophobic momentums of erasure.

I'd be curious to hear some thoughts on the challenges we face in speaking and publishing across lines of race, age, privilege, social/cultural background, gender, sexuality (and other identifiers) within the community as well as creating and maintaining safe spaces, vs. the dangers of remaining and producing in isolated "silos" and/or disciplinary and/or institutional bounds?

The notion of disciplinary (and/or institutional) "siloing" has become common parlance, yet I'd like to pause with a definitional anecdote. While a silo (from siros, cornpit) may house grain for compressed storage, many such grains are the product of eminently resource-intensive mono-cultural production. Beyond that, the silo may occur as a pit, yet it also may assume tower-form, which suggests a consolidation of power over both our atmospheric commons as well as that which is below (the decreasingly arable commons of the soil). It is from these agricultural applications that we get the idea of 'siloed' specialists, yet in the dictionary rankings of the term, between the agricultural and the specialization-linked definitions, we find something at once chilling and somehow also unsurprising: silo, an underground chamber in which a guided missile is kept ready for firing.

I hope the long anecdote is forgivable. I thought I'd follow it through here as a way of underscoring the critical value of traversing disciplinary and institutional divides. For those of us in the academy, little good can come of our institutional siloing, yet we must proceed out from our towers/pits/chambers with humility for non-institutional contexts of activism, knowledge production, and social critique. As a mid-degree PhD student, I feel especially alive to the need for comprehensive efforts to reach across these dividing lines you've specified to integrate other voices and the unique imperatives they specify and advance. While this may be easier said than done, the difficulty of both respecting safe spaces and offering avenues and points of entry for alliance and coalition-building is one to which we must respond; providing platforms for a more expansive creating, querying public is both possible and deeply necessary.

Is there anything else we should have asked, or that you want to share?

Intuition and the backward glance: I'm learning to deepen my appreciation for those proverbial wheels that have already been invented (and sometimes forgotten). I recently read Rebecca Solnit's Savage Dreams, *and in that book, she talks about her discovery of the national women's antinuclear movement that emerged in the early 1960s. Solnit admits her surprise that even amongst pacificists and feminists, radical predecessors are all too swiftly forgotten. I've taken to heart this idea of hers: "Those who don't remember history are doomed to start all over again from scratch."*

Hold closely to life-giving, justice-seeking predecessors, and scrap the rest: intuition is there as a guide. Sure, it may occasionally mislead, yet more often than not, I think intuition tends to flare toward futures that have everything to do with the past. This is important, and enables valuable commemorative work to carry demands for justice and repair into the present.

ABOUT THE AUTHOR

KNAR GAVIN attended the Iowa Writers' Workshop and is a doctoral candidate in English at the University of Pennsylvania. Her poetry has been published or is forthcoming in *AGNI, Birdfeast, Poetry, BOAAT, Caketrain, Booth, the Journal, Storm Cellar, Yemassee, Print-Oriented Bastards, Quarterly West, SoftBlow, Glittermob, Heavy Feather Review* and elsewhere. She writes the occasional folk song and rides bikes with Team Laser Cats, a Philadelphia women's cycling squad. Her tumbles can be found at knargavin.tumblr.com.

ABOUT THE COVER ART:

The Operating System 2019 chapbooks, in both digital and print, feature art from Heidi Reszies. The work is from a series entitled "Collected Objects & the Dead Birds I Did Not Carry Home," which are mixed media collages with encaustic on 8 x 8 wood panel, made in 2018.

Heidi writes: "This series explores objects/fragments of material culture--how objects occupy space, and my relationship to them or to their absence."

ABOUT THE ARTIST:

Heidi Reszies is a poet/transdisciplinary artist living in Richmond, Virginia. Her visual art is included in the National Museum of Women in the Arts CLARA Database of Women Artists. She teaches letterpress printing at the Virginia Commonwealth University School of the Arts, and is the creator/curator of Artifact Press. Her poetry collection titled *Illusory Borders* is forthcoming from The Operating System in 2019, and now available for pre-order. Her collection titled *Of Water & Other Soft Constructions* was selected by Samiya Bashir as the winner of the Anhinga Press 2018 Robert Dana Prize for Poetry (forthcoming in 2019).

Find her at heidireszies.com

WHY PRINT DOCUMENT?

The Operating System uses the language "print document" to differentiate from the book-object as part of our mission to distinguish the act of documentation-in-book-FORM from the act of publishing as a backwards-facing replication of the book's agentive *role* as it may have appeared the last several centuries of its history. Ultimately, I approach the book as TECHNOLOGY: one of a variety of printed documents (in this case, bound) that humans have invented and in turn used to archive and disseminate ideas, beliefs, stories, and other evidence of production.

Ownership and use of printing presses and access to (or restriction of printed materials) has long been a site of struggle, related in many ways to revolutionary activity and the fight for civil rights and free speech all over the world. While (in many countries) the contemporary quotidian landscape has indeed drastically shifted in its access to platforms for sharing information and in the widespread ability to "publish" digitally, even with extremely limited resources, the importance of publication on physical media has not diminished. In fact, this may be the most critical time in recent history for activist groups, artists, and others to insist upon learning, establishing, and encouraging personal and community documentation practices. Hear me out.

With The OS's print endeavors I wanted to open up a conversation about this: the ultimately radical, transgressive act of creating PRINT /DOCUMENTATION in the digital age. It's a question of the archive, and of history: who gets to tell the story, and what evidence of our life, our behaviors, our experiences are we leaving behind? We can know little to nothing about the future into which we're leaving an unprecedentedly digital document trail — but we can be assured that publications, government agencies, museums, schools, and other institutional powers that be will continue to leave BOTH a digital and print version of their production for the official record. Will we?

As a (rogue) anthropologist and long time academic, I can easily pull up many accounts about how lives, behaviors, experiences — how THE STORY of a time or place — was pieced together using the deep study of correspondence, notebooks, and other physical documents which are no longer the norm in many lives and practices. As we move our creative behaviors towards digital note taking, and even audio and video, what can we predict about future technology that is in any way assuring that our stories will be accurately told – or told at all? How will we leave these things for the record?

In these documents we say: WE WERE HERE, WE EXISTED, WE HAVE A DIFFERENT STORY

- Lynne DeSilva-Johnson [ELÆ], Founder/Managing Editor,
THE OPERATING SYSTEM, Brooklyn NY 2019

PLEASE SEE OUR FULL CATALOG
FOR FULL LENGTH VOLUMES AND PREVIOUS CHAPBOOK SERIES:
HTTPS://SQUAREUP.COM/STORE/THE-OPERATING-SYSTEM/

THE 2019 SERIES MARKS OUR 7TH AND FINAL SPRING 4-BOOK SERIES
THANK YOU TO ALL THE WONDERFUL CREATORS BEHIND THESE TITLES

CHAPBOOK SERIES 2018 : TALES
Greater Grave - Jacq Greyja; Needles of Itching Feathers - Jared Schlickling;
Want-Catcher - Adra Raine; We, The Monstrous - Mark DuCharme

CHAPBOOK SERIES 2017 : INCANTATIONS
featuring original cover art by Barbara Byers
sp. - Susan Charkes; Radio Poems - Jeffrey Cyphers Wright;
Fixing a Witch/Hexing the Stitch - Jacklyn Janeksela;
cosmos a personal voyage by carl sagan ann druyan steven sotor and me - Connie Mae Oliver

CHAPBOOK SERIES 2016: OF SOUND MIND
*featuring the quilt drawings of Daphne Taylor
Improper Maps - Alex Crowley; While Listening - Alaina Ferris;
Chords - Peter Longofono; Any Seam or Needlework - Stanford Cheung

CHAPBOOK SERIES 2015: OF SYSTEMS OF
*featuring original cover art by Emma Steinkraus
Cyclorama - Davy Knittle; The Sensitive Boy Slumber Party Manifesto - Joseph
Cuillier; Neptune Court - Anton Yakovlev; Schema - Anurak Saelow

CHAPBOOK SERIES 2014: BY HAND
Pull, A Ballad - Maryam Parhizkar;
Can You See that Sound - Jeff Musillo
Executive Producer Chris Carter - Peter Milne Greiner;
Spooky Action at a Distance - Gregory Crosby;

CHAPBOOK SERIES 2013: WOODBLOCK
*featuring original prints from Kevin William Reed
Strange Coherence - Bill Considine; The Sword of Things - Tony Hoffman;
Talk About Man Proof - Lancelot Runge / John Kropa;
An Admission as a Warning Against the Value of Our Conclusions -Alexis Quinlan

DOC U MENT
/däkyəmənt/

First meant "instruction" or "evidence," whether written or not.

noun - a piece of written, printed, or electronic matter that provides information or evidence or that serves as an official record
verb - record (something) in written, photographic, or other form
synonyms - paper - deed - record - writing - act - instrument

[*Middle English, precept, from Old French, from Latin documentum, example, proof, from docre, to teach; see dek- in Indo-European roots.*]

Who is responsible for the manufacture of value?

Based on what supercilious ontology have we landed in a space where we vie against other creative people in vain pursuit of the fleeting credibilities of the scarcity economy, rather than freely collaborating and sharing openly with each other in ecstatic celebration of MAKING?

While we understand and acknowledge the economic pressures and fear-mongering that threatens to dominate and crush the creative impulse, we also believe that ***now more than ever we have the tools to relinquish agency via cooperative means,*** fueled by the fires of the Open Source Movement.

Looking out across the invisible vistas of that rhizomatic parallel country we can begin to see our community beyond constraints, in the place where intention meets resilient, proactive, collaborative organization.

Here is a document born of that belief, sown purely of imagination and will.
When we document we assert. We print to make real, to reify our being there.
When we do so with mindful intention to address our process, to open our work to others, to create beauty in words in space, to respect and acknowledge the strength of the page we now hold physical, a thing in our hand… we remind ourselves that, like Dorothy: *we had the power all along, my dears.*

THE PRINT! DOCUMENT SERIES
is a project of
the trouble with bartleby
in collaboration with
the operating system